GRAPHIC HISTORY

THE BATTLE OF THE

ALAMO

by Matt Doeden

illustrated by Charles Barnett III
and Phil Miller

Consultant:
Sally Koch
Assistant Coordinator of Educational Programs
The Alamo, San Antonio, Texas

Capstone
press

Mankato, Minnesota

Graphic Library is published by Capstone Press,
1710 Roe Crest Drive, North Mankato, Minnesota 56003.
www.capstonepub.com

 Books published by Capstone Press are manufactured with paper
containing at least 10 percent post-consumer waste.

Library of Congress Cataloging-in-Publication Data
Doeden, Matt.
  The Battle of the Alamo / by Matt Doeden; illustrated by Charles Barnett, III. and
    Phil Miller
    p. cm.—(Graphic library. Graphic history)
    Includes bibliographical references and index.
    ISBN-13: 978-0-7368-3832-0 (hardcover)   ISBN-10: 0-7368-3832-5 (hardcover)
    ISBN-13: 978-0-7368-5242-5 (softcover pbk.)   ISBN-10: 0-7368-5242-5 (softcover pbk.)
    1. Alamo (San Antonio, Tex.)—Siege, 1836—Juvenile literature. I. Barnett, Charles, III.
    and Phil Miller. II. Title. III. Series.
F390.D64 2005
976.4'03—dc22   2004014483

Summary: The story of the 1836 Battle of the Alamo is told in a graphic-novel format.

Editor's note: Direct quotations from primary sources are indicated by a yellow background.

Direct quotations appear on the following pages:
Page 5, from *The Fall of the Alamo*, the personal account of Dr. John Sutherland taken from
  Texas A&M Digital Library (http://dl.tamu.edu/Projects/sodct/sthland1.htm).
Page 8, letter of William Travis dated February 24, 1836, taken from Texas State Library and
  Archives Commission (http://www.tsl.state.tx.us/treasures/republic/alamo/travis-about.html).
Page 13, letter of William Travis to David Ayers dated March 3, 1836, provided by Sally Koch,
  Assistant Coordinator of Educational Programs at the Alamo in San Antonio, Texas.
Page 14, Translation of Santa Anna's formal written orders to troops dated March 5, 1836, from
  Texas A&M Digital Library (http://dl.tamu.edu/Projects/sodct/dewitt.htm).
Page 17, Account of Travis' slave, Joe, taken from *Duel of Eagles: the Mexican and U.S. fight for
  the Alamo* by Jeff Long (New York: Morrow, 1990).
Page 27, Sam Houston's speech taken from *Eighteen Minutes: The Battle of San Jacinto and the
  Texas Independence Campaign* by Stephen L. Moore (Dallas: Republic of Texas Press, 2004).

Credits   **Acknowledgments**

Art Directors   **Editor**   Capstone Press thanks Philip Charles
Jason Knudson   Heather Adamson   Crawford, Library Director, Essex High
Heather Kindseth   School, Essex, Vermont, and columnist for
                           Colorist   *Knowledge Quest*, for his assistance in the
Storyboard Artist   Brent Schoonover   preparation of this book.
Keith Wilson
                                             Special thanks to Charles Barnett III and
                                             Phil Miller at Cavalier Graphics.

Printed in the United States of America in Stevens Point, Wisconsin.
042013
007323R

TABLE ✦✦✦ OF CONTENTS

CHAPTER 1

SURRENDER ★★★ OR DIE

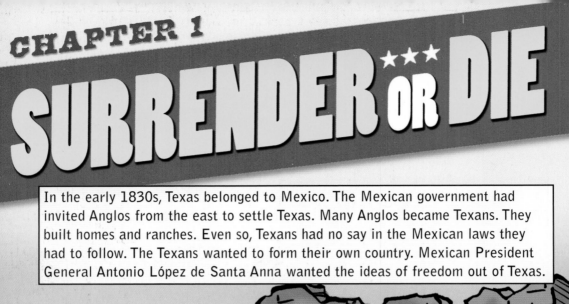

In the early 1830s, Texas belonged to Mexico. The Mexican government had invited Anglos from the east to settle Texas. Many Anglos became Texans. They built homes and ranches. Even so, Texans had no say in the Mexican laws they had to follow. The Texans wanted to form their own country. Mexican President General Antonio López de Santa Anna wanted the ideas of freedom out of Texas.

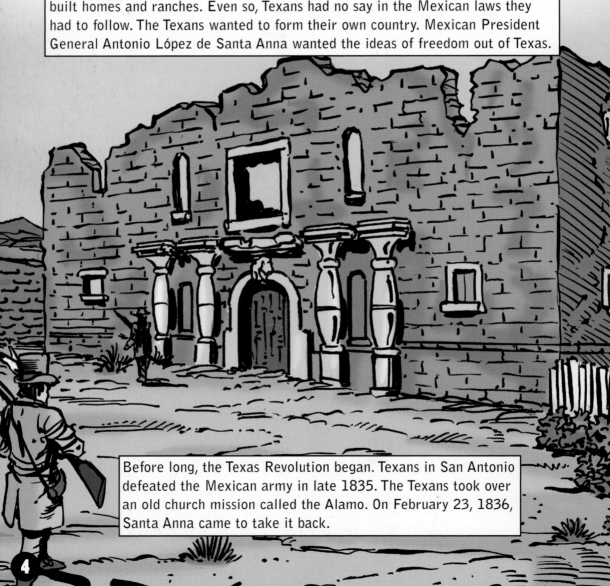

Before long, the Texas Revolution began. Texans in San Antonio defeated the Mexican army in late 1835. The Texans took over an old church mission called the Alamo. On February 23, 1836, Santa Anna came to take it back.

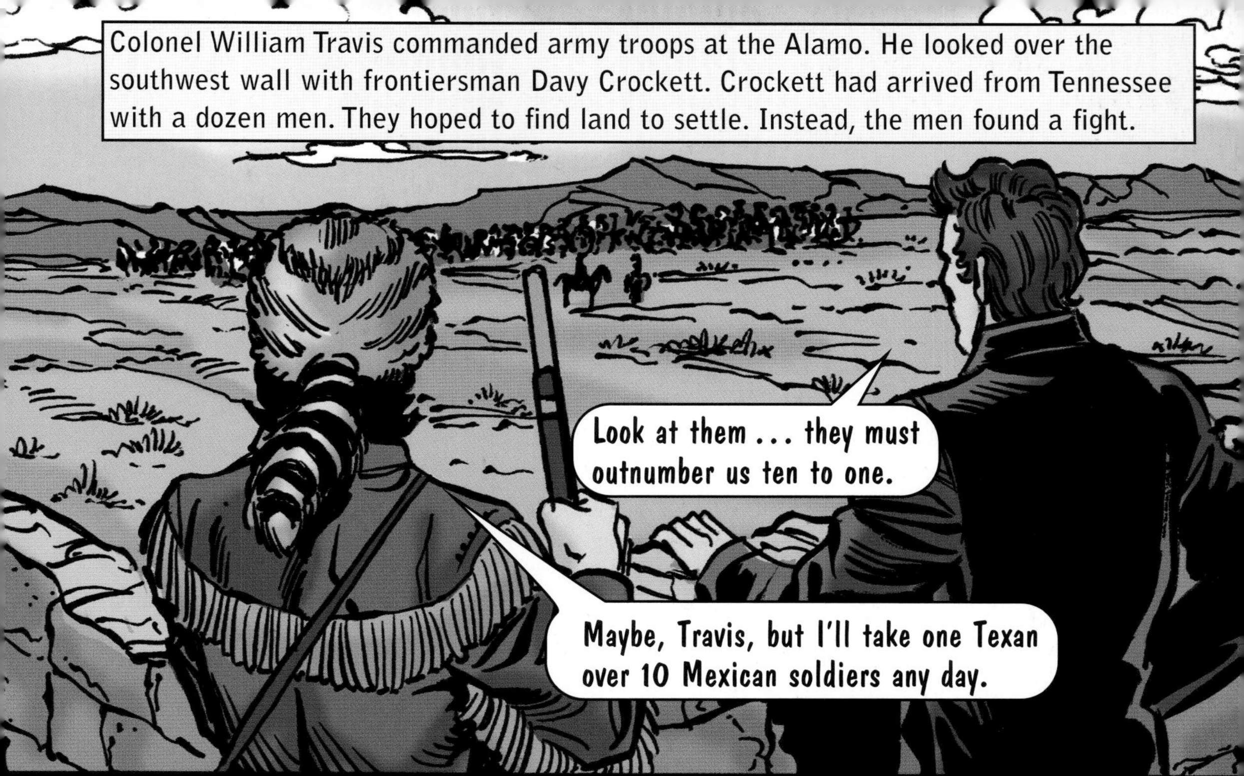
Colonel William Travis commanded army troops at the Alamo. He looked over the southwest wall with frontiersman Davy Crockett. Crockett had arrived from Tennessee with a dozen men. They hoped to find land to settle. Instead, the men found a fight.
Look at them . . . they must outnumber us ten to one.
Maybe, Travis, but I'll take one Texan over 10 Mexican soldiers any day.

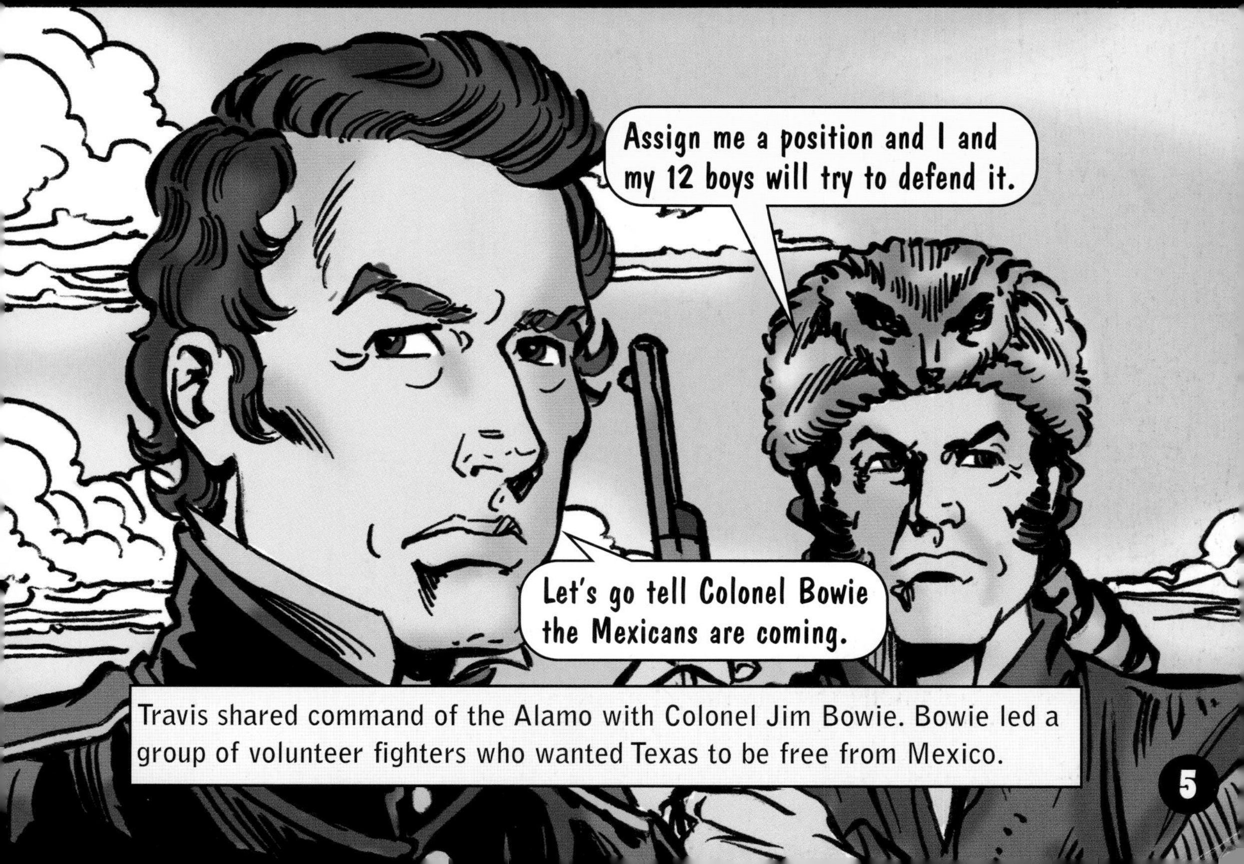
Assign me a position and I and my 12 boys will try to defend it.
Let's go tell Colonel Bowie the Mexicans are coming.
Travis shared command of the Alamo with Colonel Jim Bowie. Bowie led a group of volunteer fighters who wanted Texas to be free from Mexico.

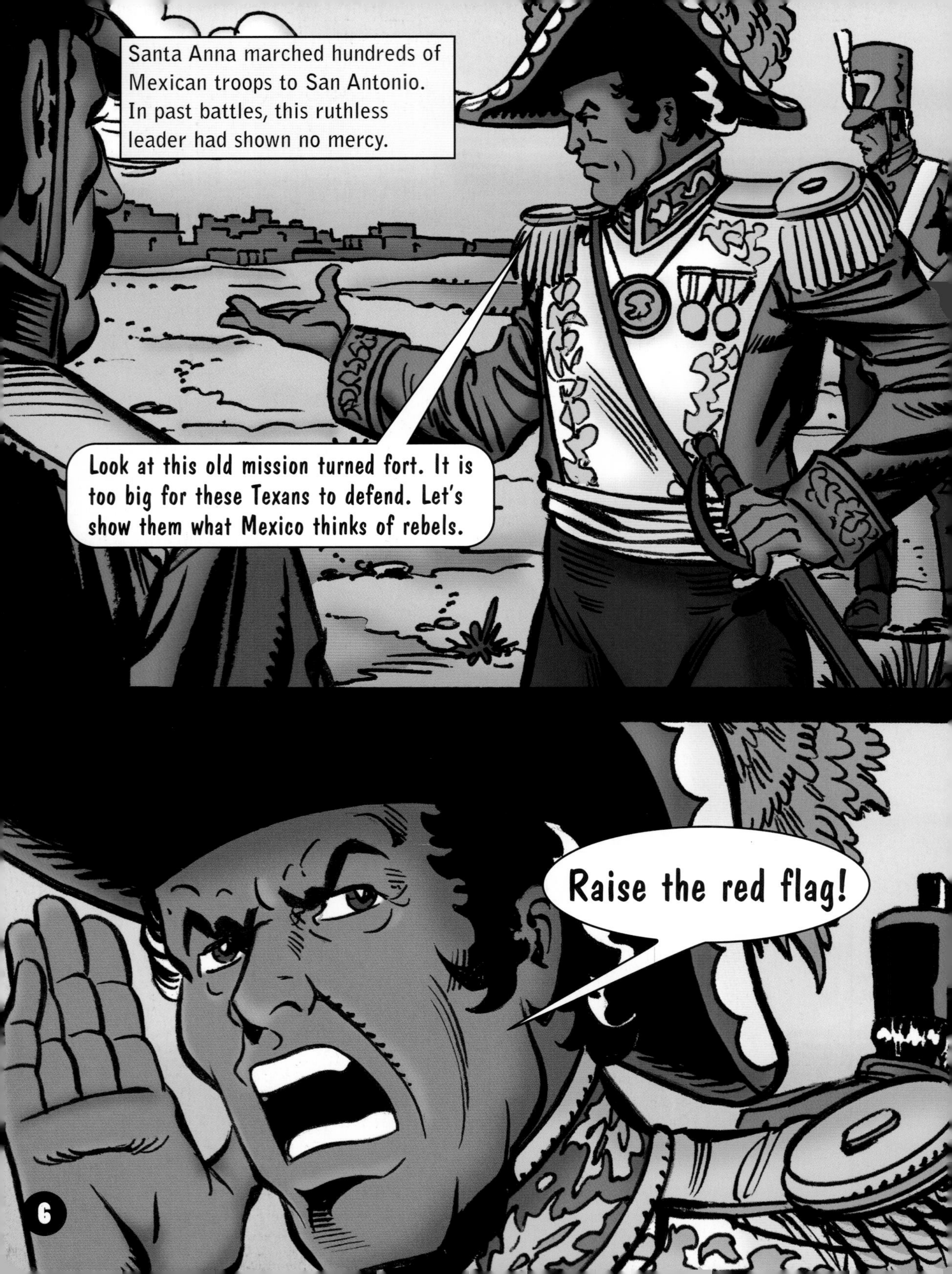

Santa Anna marched hundreds of Mexican troops to San Antonio. In past battles, this ruthless leader had shown no mercy.
Look at this old mission turned fort. It is too big for these Texans to defend. Let's show them what Mexico thinks of rebels.
Raise the red flag!

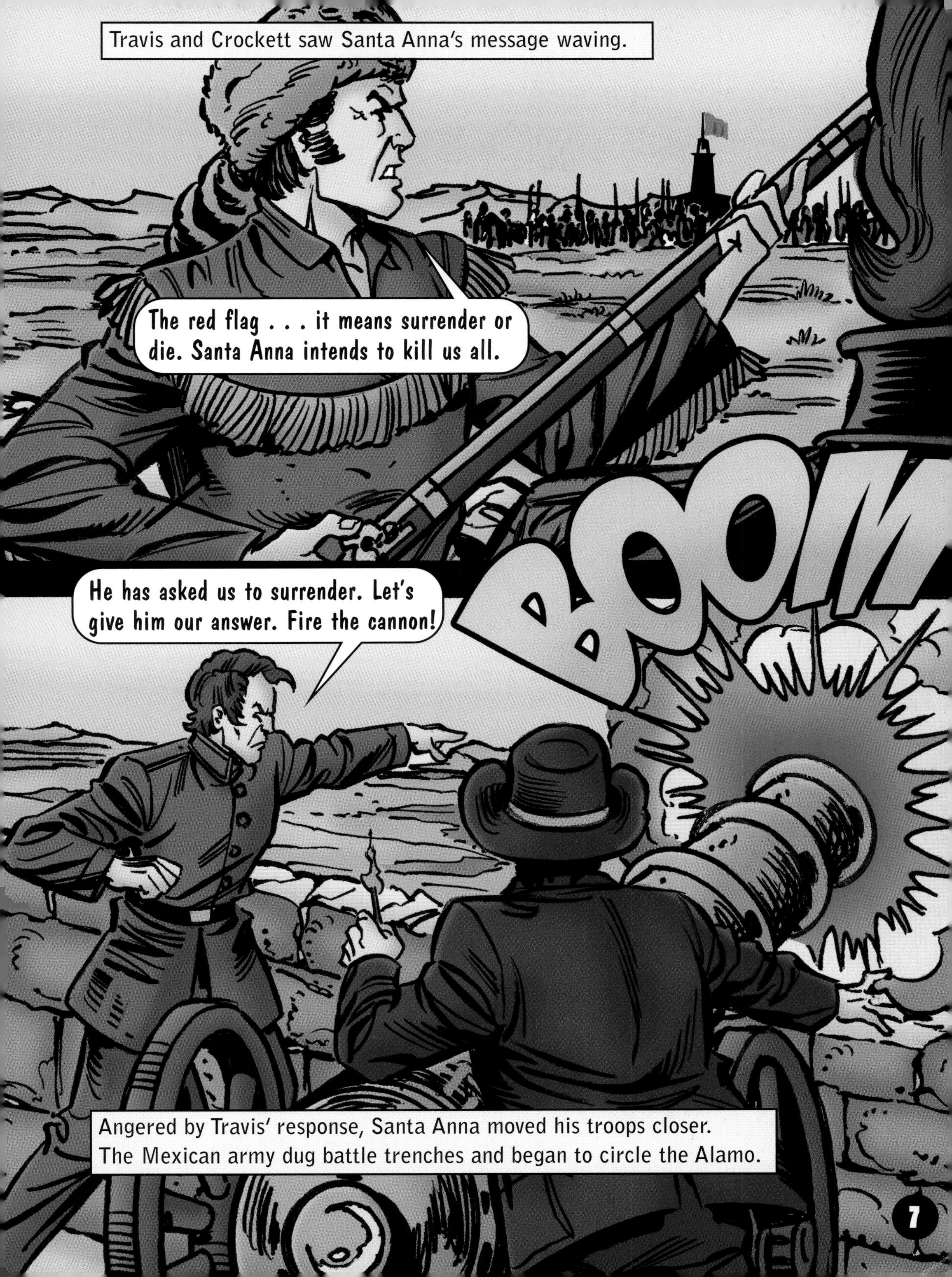
Travis and Crockett saw Santa Anna's message waving.
The red flag . . . it means surrender or die. Santa Anna intends to kill us all.
He has asked us to surrender. Let's give him our answer. Fire the cannon!
BOOM
Angered by Travis' response, Santa Anna moved his troops closer. The Mexican army dug battle trenches and began to circle the Alamo.

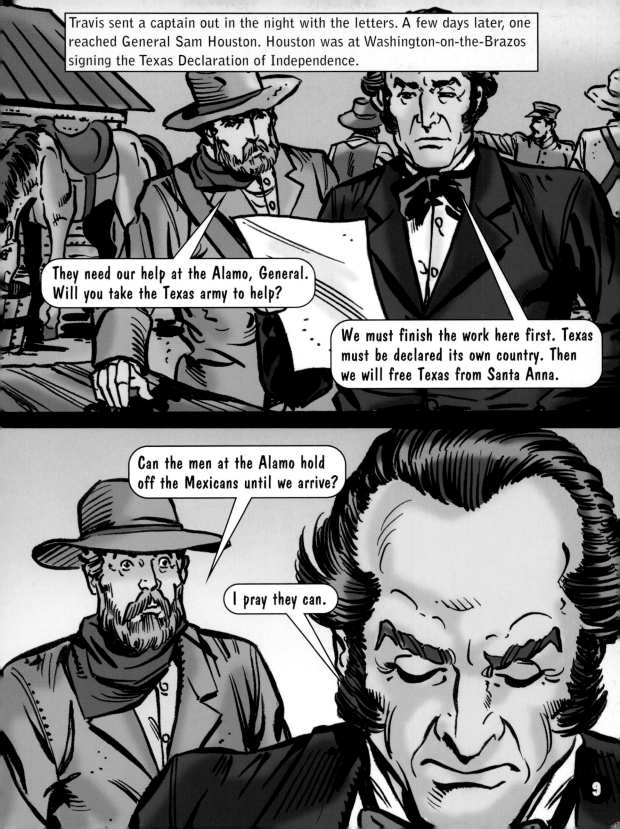

CHAPTER 2
THE SIEGE

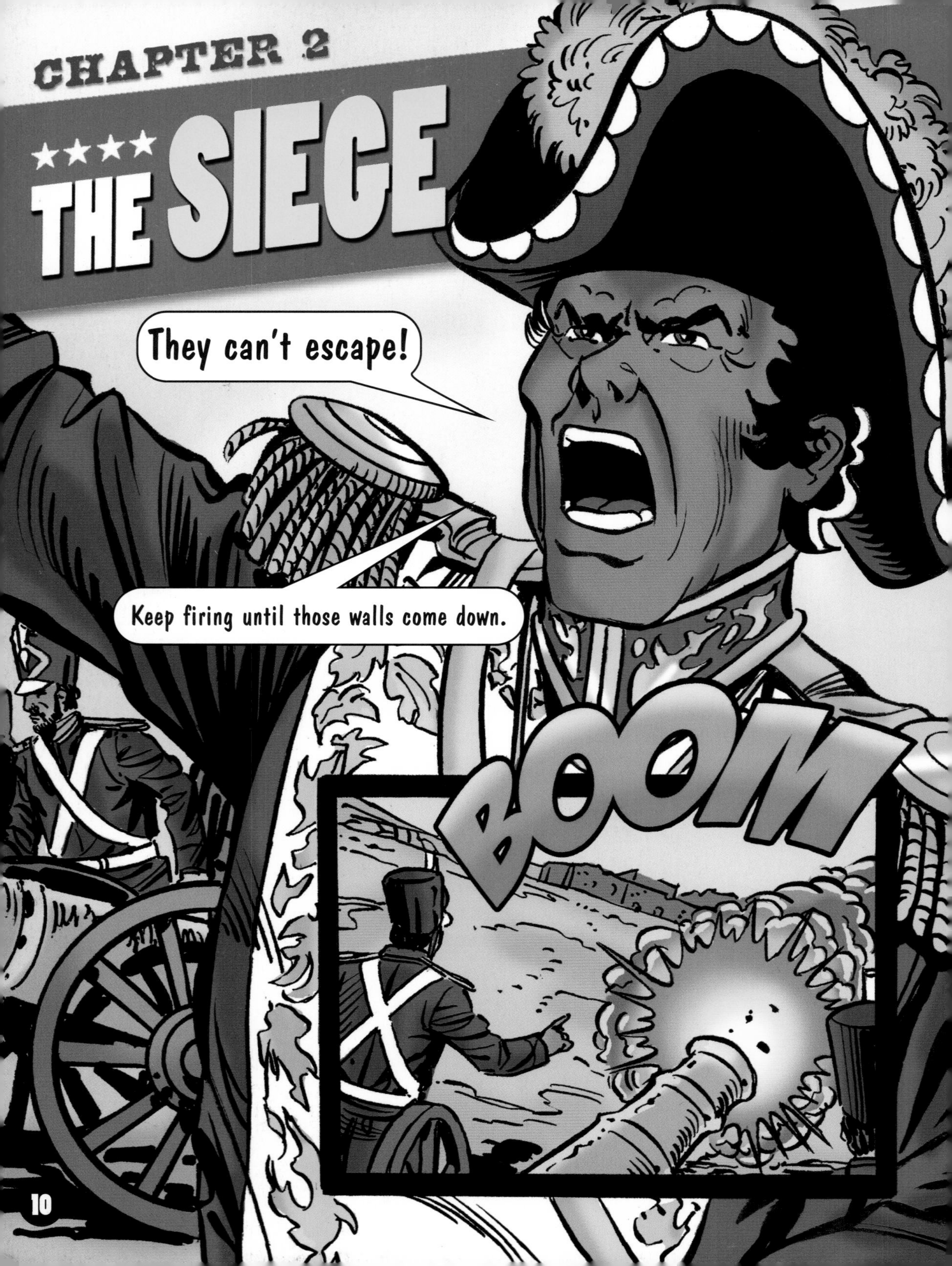
They can't escape!
Keep firing until those walls come down.
BOOM

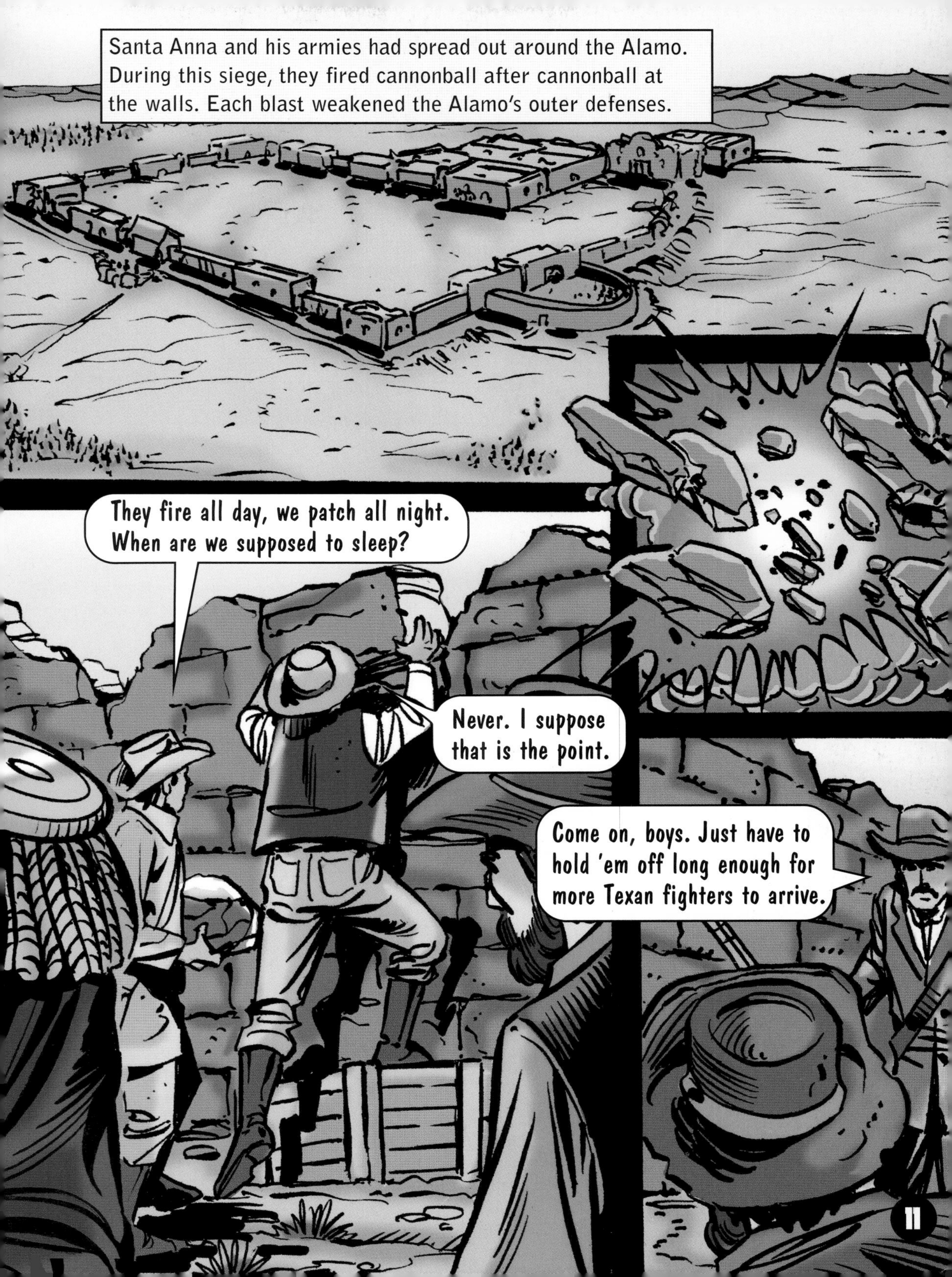
Santa Anna and his armies had spread out around the Alamo. During this siege, they fired cannonball after cannonball at the walls. Each blast weakened the Alamo's outer defenses.
They fire all day, we patch all night. When are we supposed to sleep?
Never. I suppose that is the point.
Come on, boys. Just have to hold 'em off long enough for more Texan fighters to arrive.

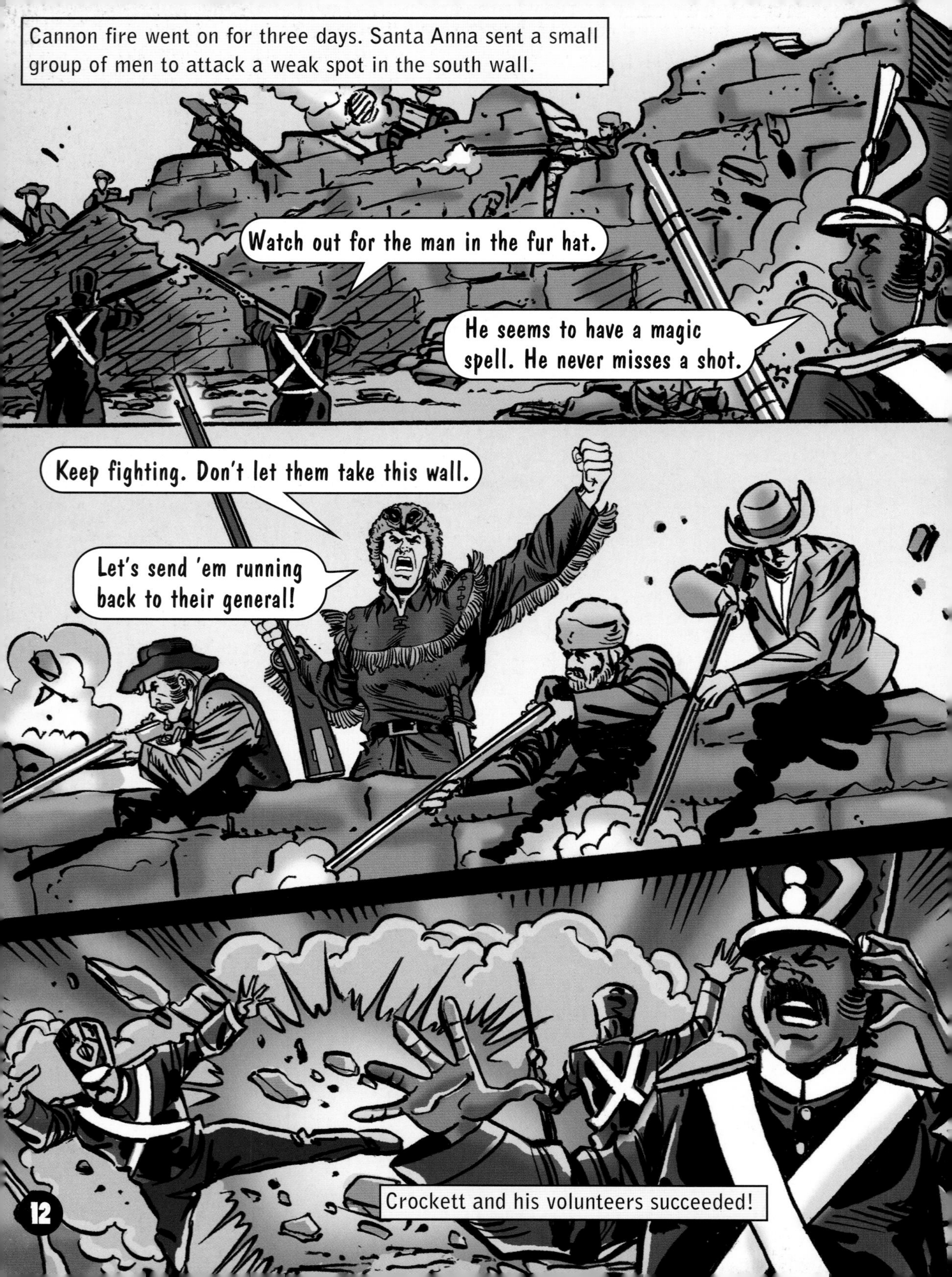

Cannon fire went on for three days. Santa Anna sent a small group of men to attack a weak spot in the south wall.
Watch out for the man in the fur hat.
He seems to have a magic spell. He never misses a shot.
Keep fighting. Don't let them take this wall.
Let's send 'em running back to their general!
Crockett and his volunteers succeeded!

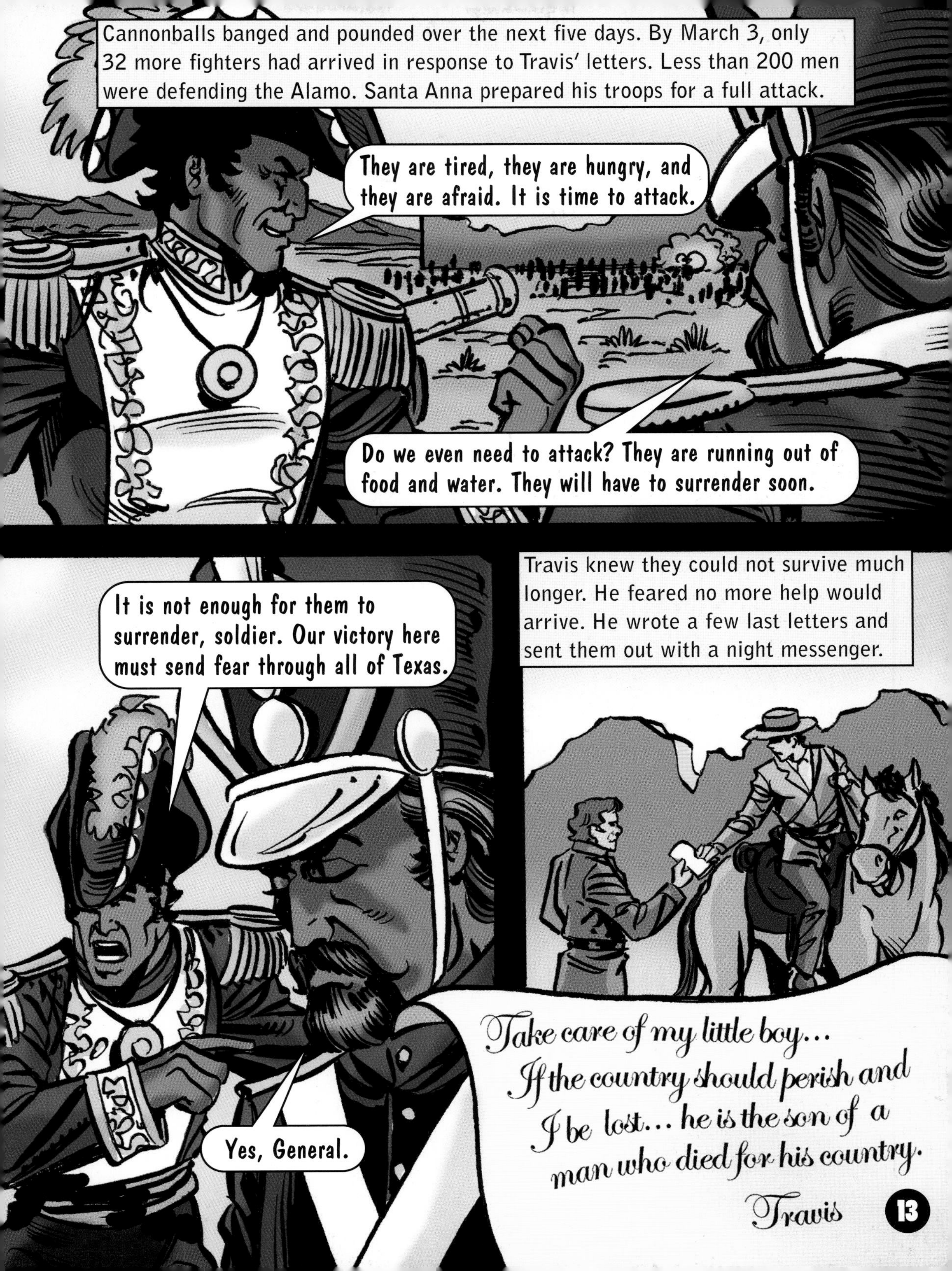
Cannonballs banged and pounded over the next five days. By March 3, only 32 more fighters had arrived in response to Travis' letters. Less than 200 men were defending the Alamo. Santa Anna prepared his troops for a full attack.
They are tired, they are hungry, and they are afraid. It is time to attack.
Do we even need to attack? They are running out of food and water. They will have to surrender soon.
It is not enough for them to surrender, soldier. Our victory here must send fear through all of Texas.
Yes, General.
Travis knew they could not survive much longer. He feared no more help would arrive. He wrote a few last letters and sent them out with a night messenger.
Take care of my little boy... If the country should perish and I be lost... he is the son of a man who died for his country.
Travis

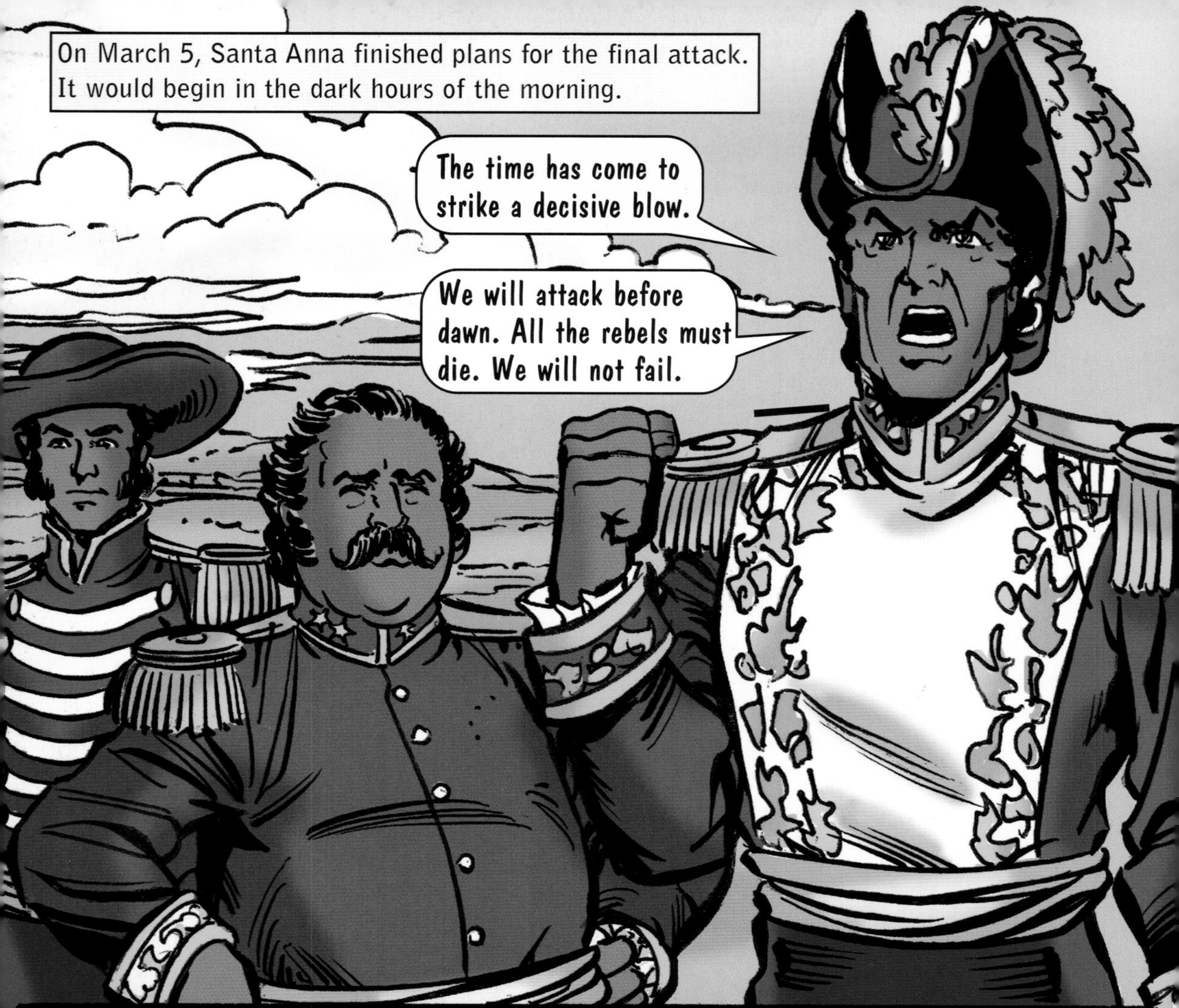
On March 5, Santa Anna finished plans for the final attack. It would begin in the dark hours of the morning.
The time has come to strike a decisive blow.
We will attack before dawn. All the rebels must die. We will not fail.

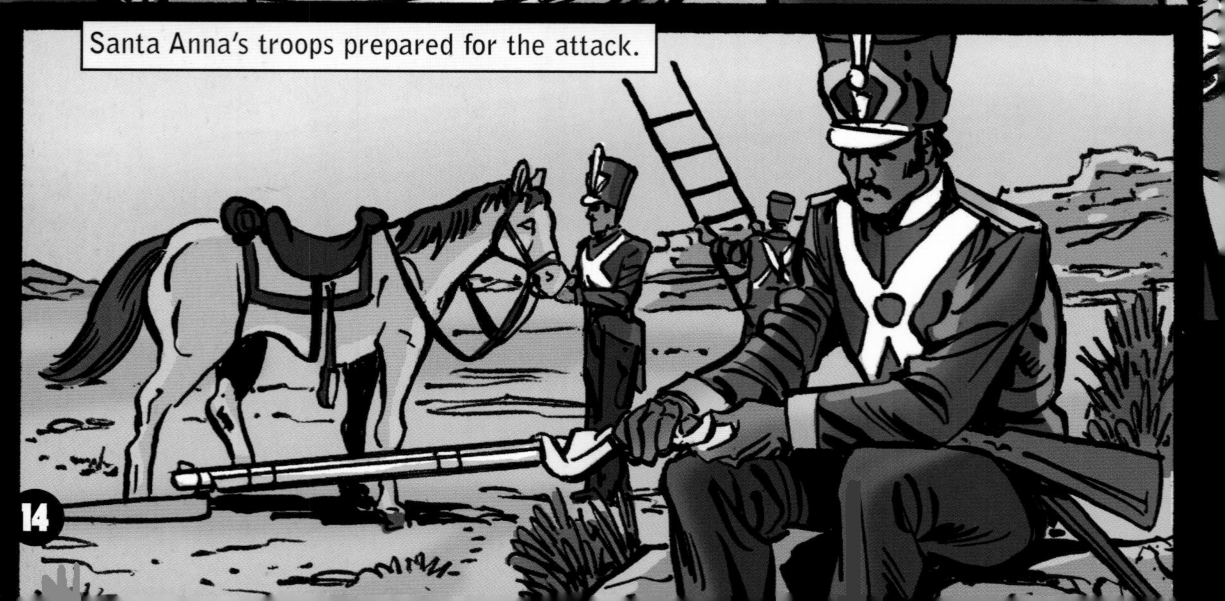
Santa Anna's troops prepared for the attack.

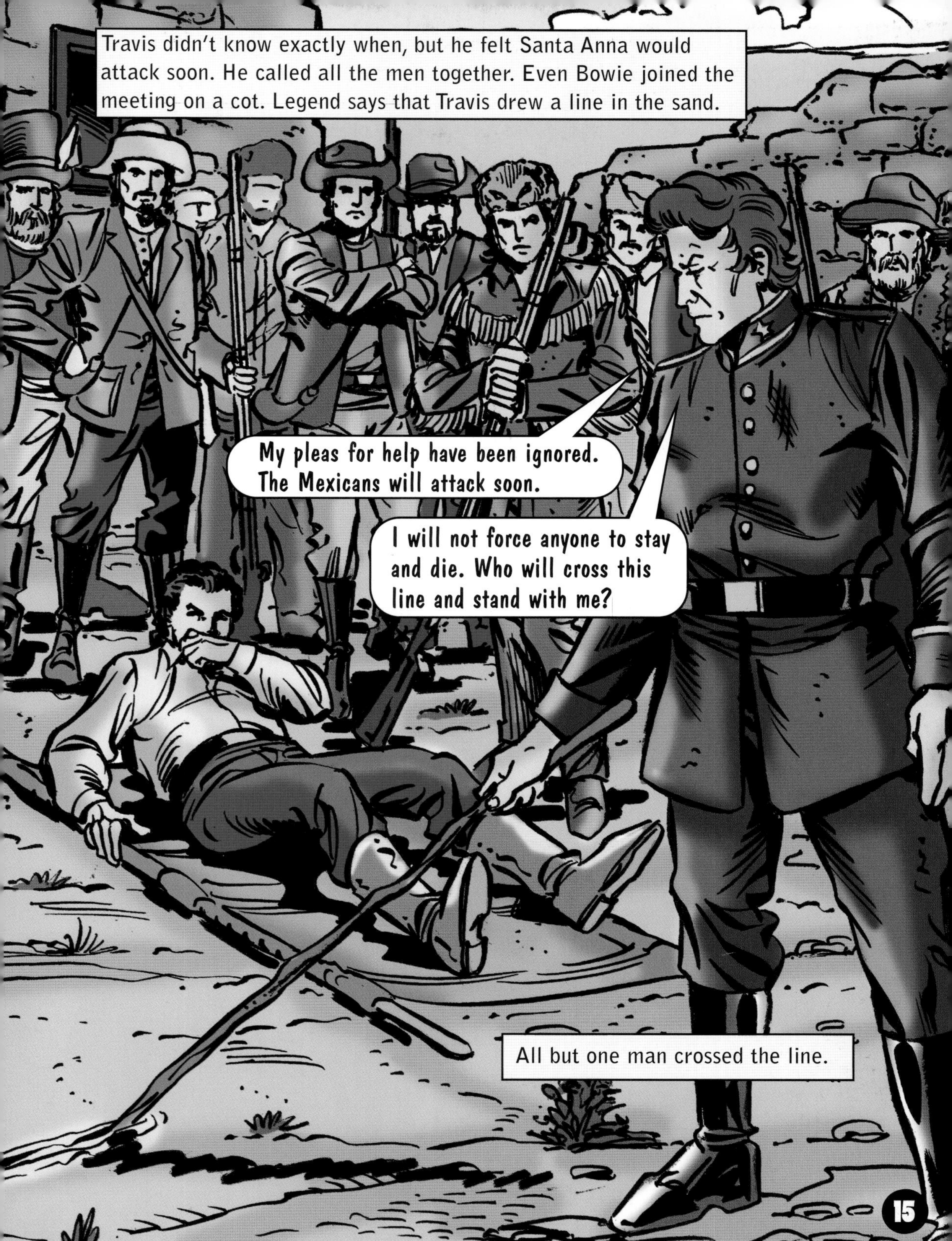
Travis didn't know exactly when, but he felt Santa Anna would attack soon. He called all the men together. Even Bowie joined the meeting on a cot. Legend says that Travis drew a line in the sand.
My pleas for help have been ignored. The Mexicans will attack soon.
I will not force anyone to stay and die. Who will cross this line and stand with me?
All but one man crossed the line.

CHAPTER 3

THE FINAL BATTLE BEGINS

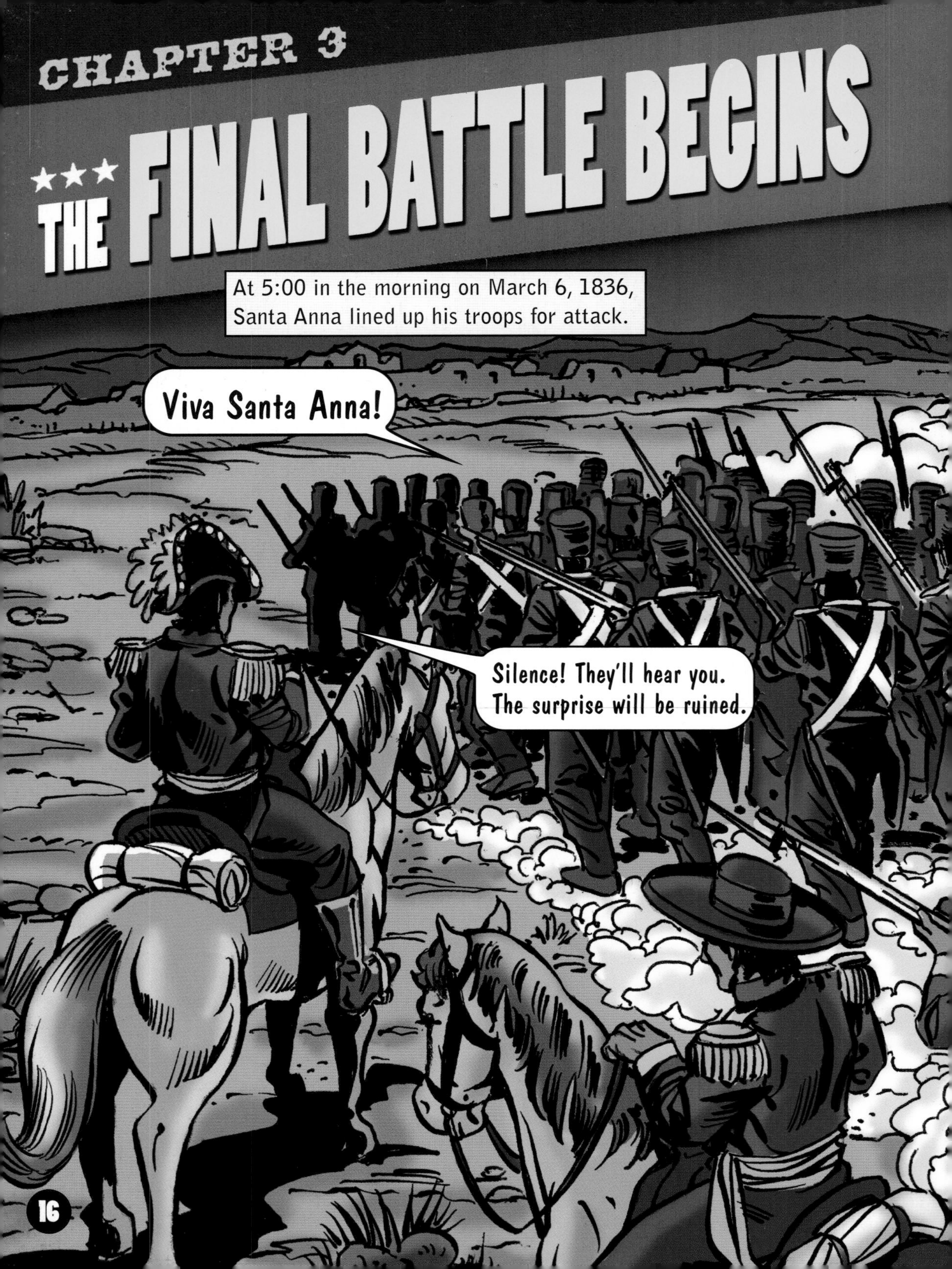

At 5:00 in the morning on March 6, 1836, Santa Anna lined up his troops for attack.
Viva Santa Anna!
Silence! They'll hear you. The surprise will be ruined.

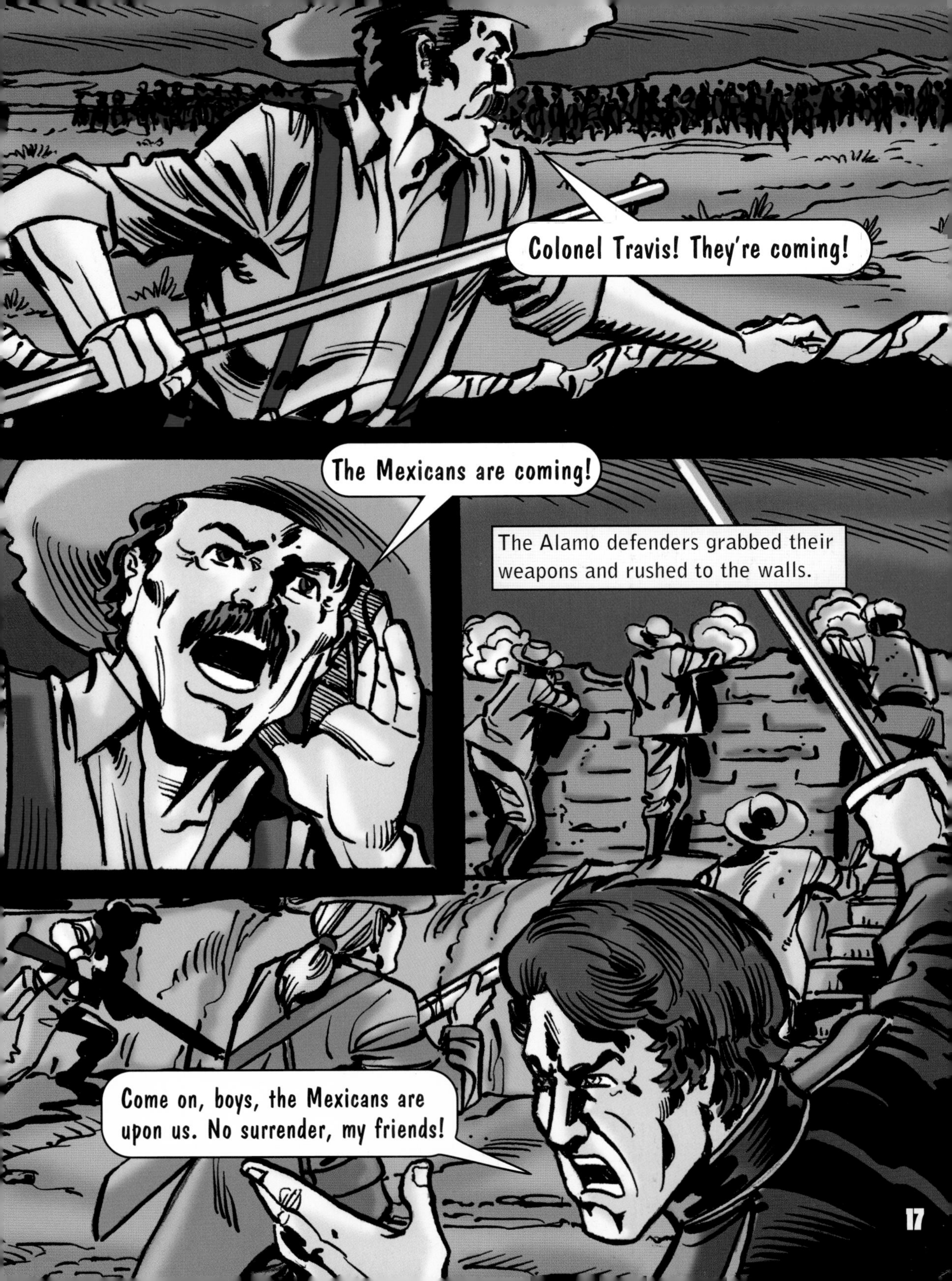

Colonel Travis! They're coming!
The Mexicans are coming!
The Alamo defenders grabbed their weapons and rushed to the walls.
Come on, boys, the Mexicans are upon us. No surrender, my friends!

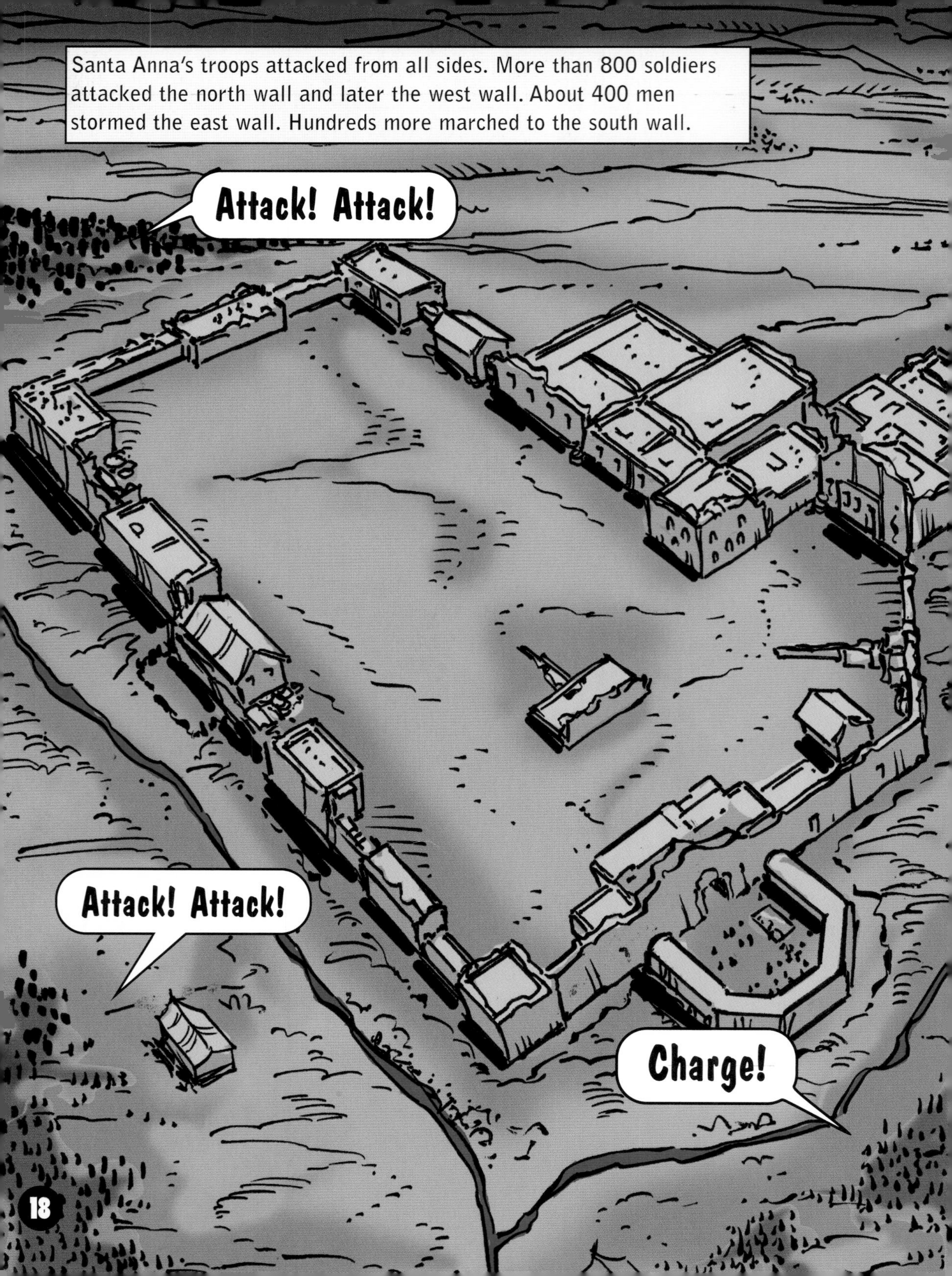
Santa Anna's troops attacked from all sides. More than 800 soldiers attacked the north wall and later the west wall. About 400 men stormed the east wall. Hundreds more marched to the south wall.
Attack! Attack!
Attack! Attack!
Charge!

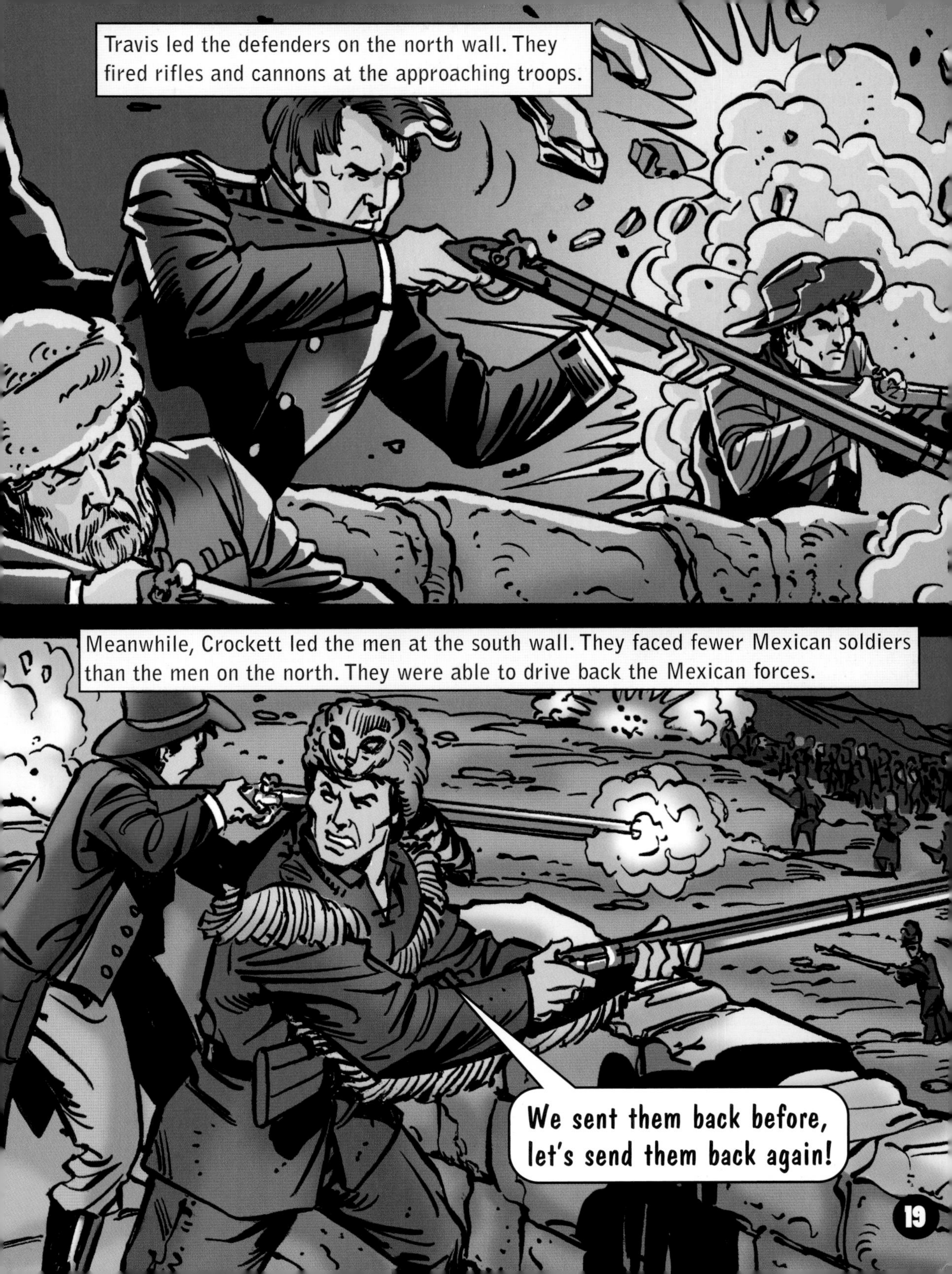
Travis led the defenders on the north wall. They fired rifles and cannons at the approaching troops.
Meanwhile, Crockett led the men at the south wall. They faced fewer Mexican soldiers than the men on the north. They were able to drive back the Mexican forces.
We sent them back before, let's send them back again!

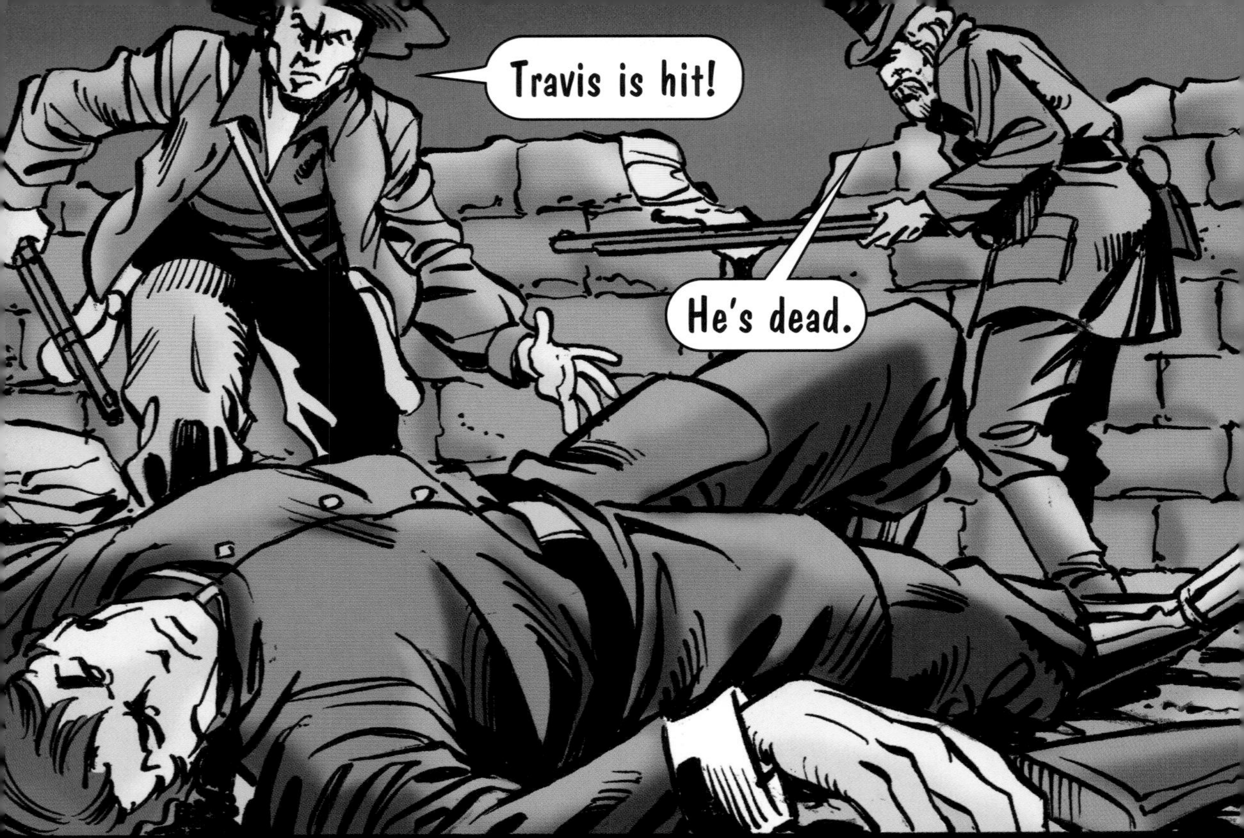
Travis is hit!
He's dead.

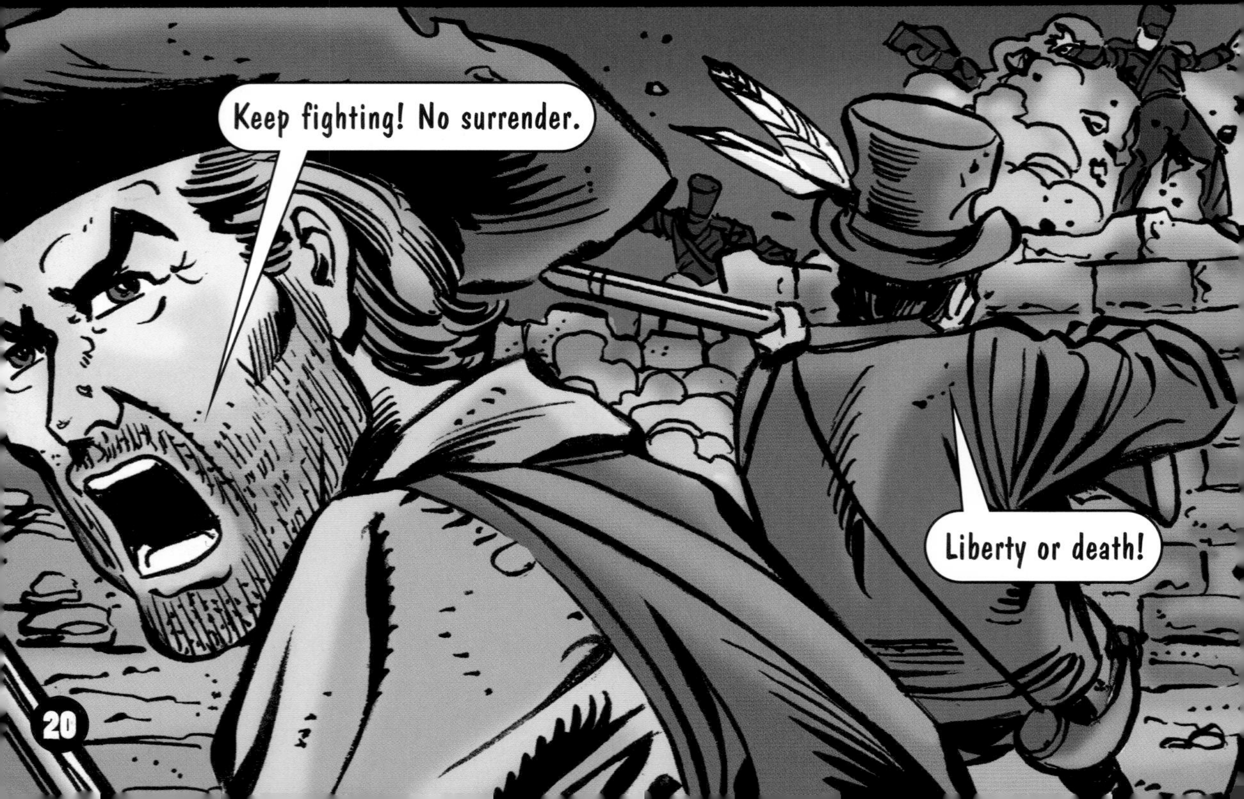
Keep fighting! No surrender.
Liberty or death!

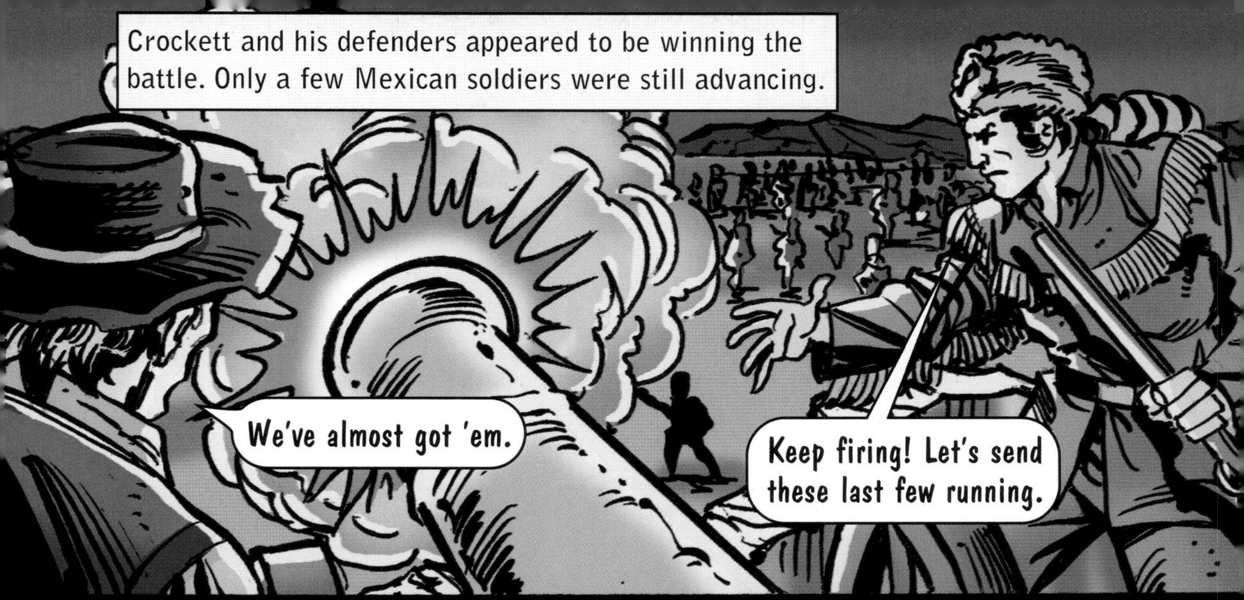
Crockett and his defenders appeared to be winning the battle. Only a few Mexican soldiers were still advancing.
We've almost got 'em.
Keep firing! Let's send these last few running.

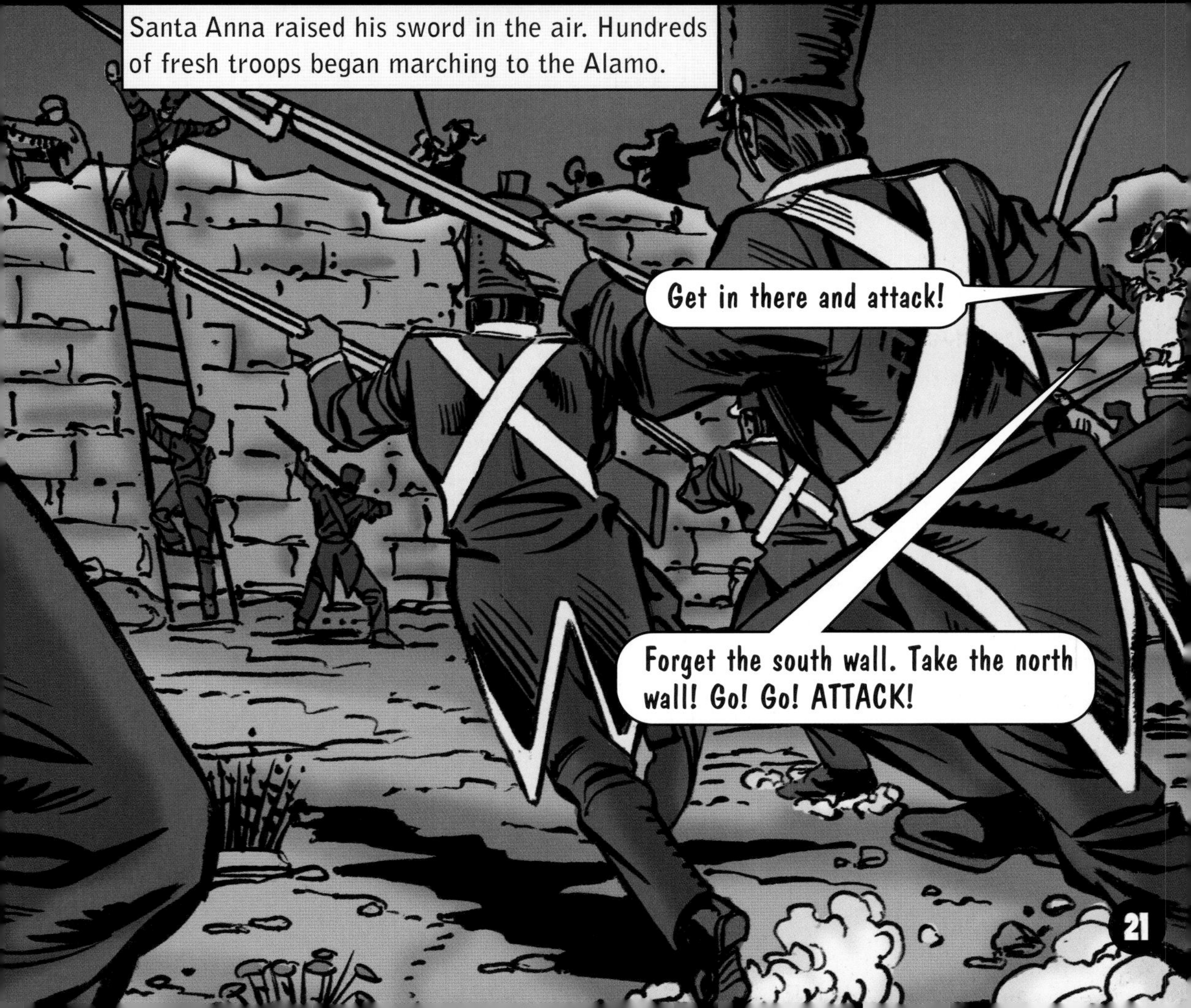
Santa Anna raised his sword in the air. Hundreds of fresh troops began marching to the Alamo.
Get in there and attack!
Forget the south wall. Take the north wall! Go! Go! ATTACK!

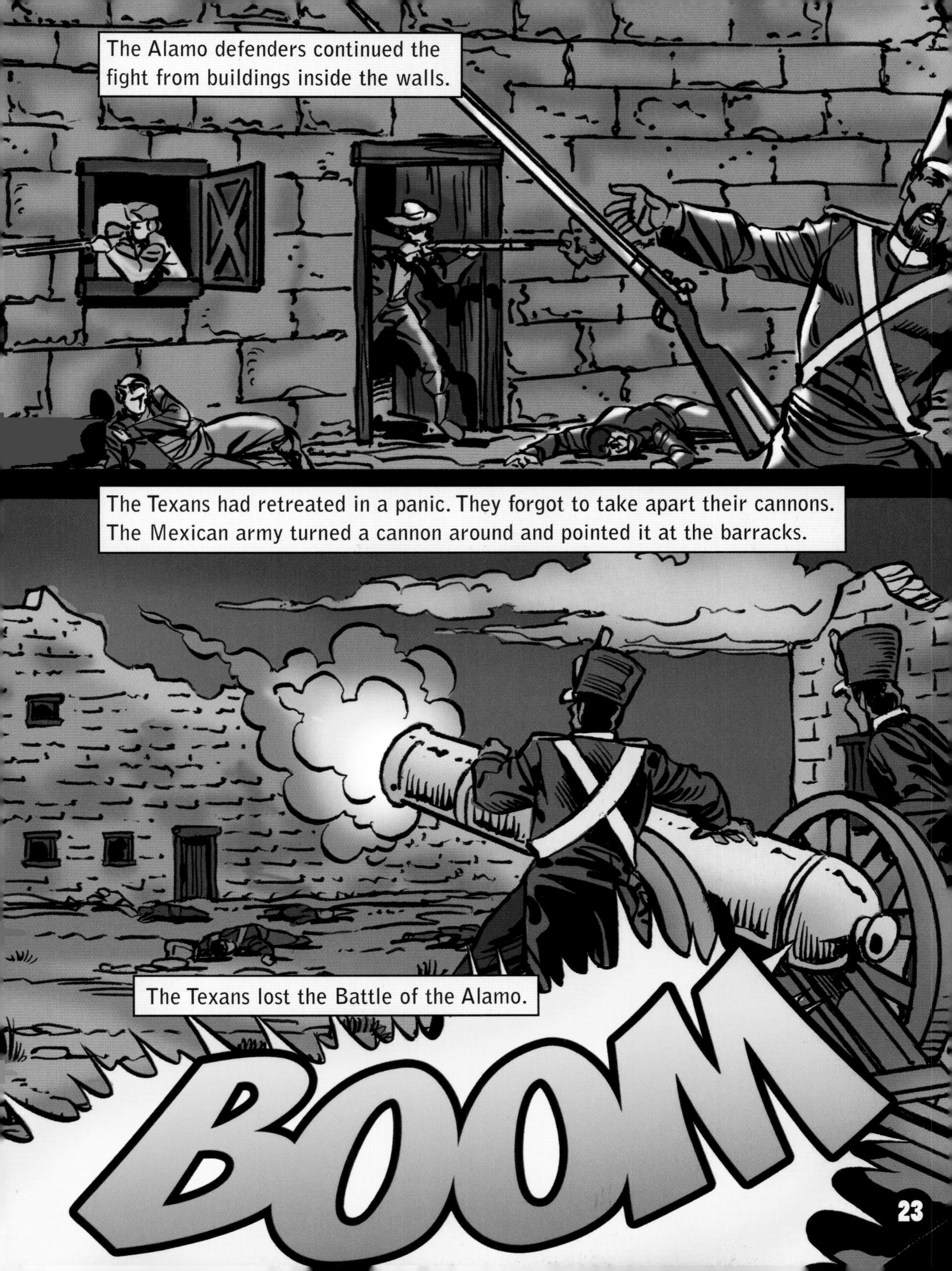
The Alamo defenders continued the fight from buildings inside the walls.
The Texans had retreated in a panic. They forgot to take apart their cannons. The Mexican army turned a cannon around and pointed it at the barracks.
The Texans lost the Battle of the Alamo.
BOOM

CHAPTER 4

THE ALAMO FALLS

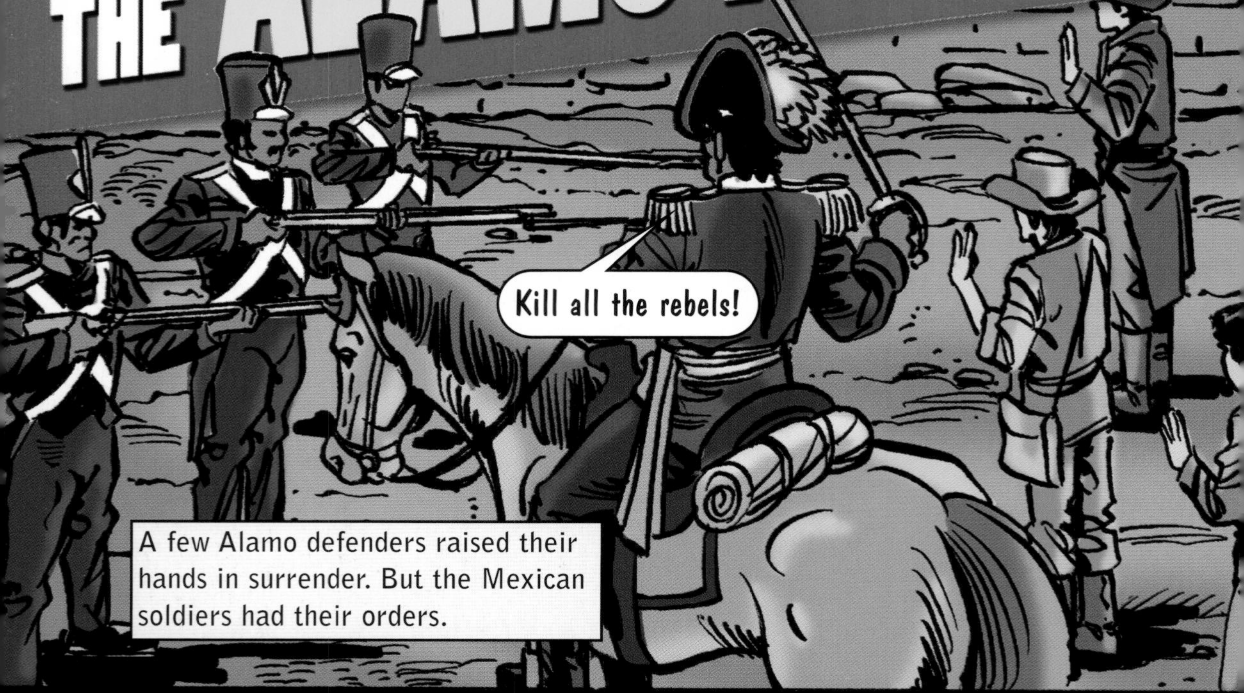
Kill all the rebels!
A few Alamo defenders raised their hands in surrender. But the Mexican soldiers had their orders.

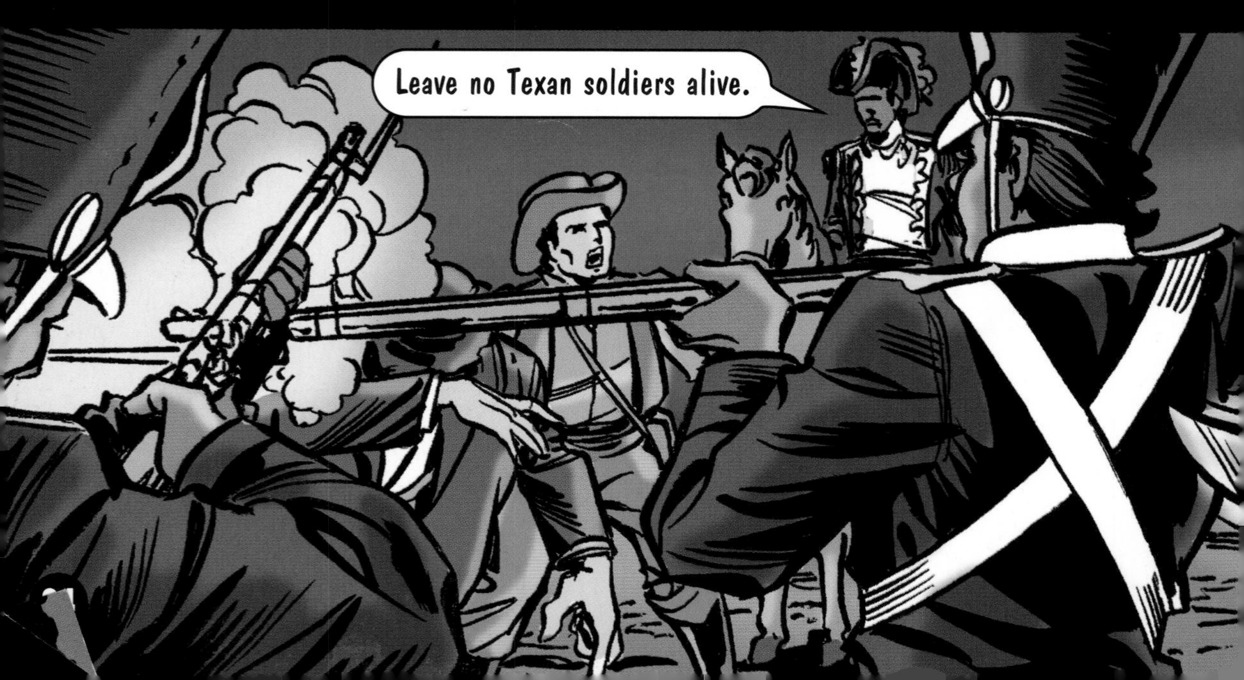
Leave no Texan soldiers alive.

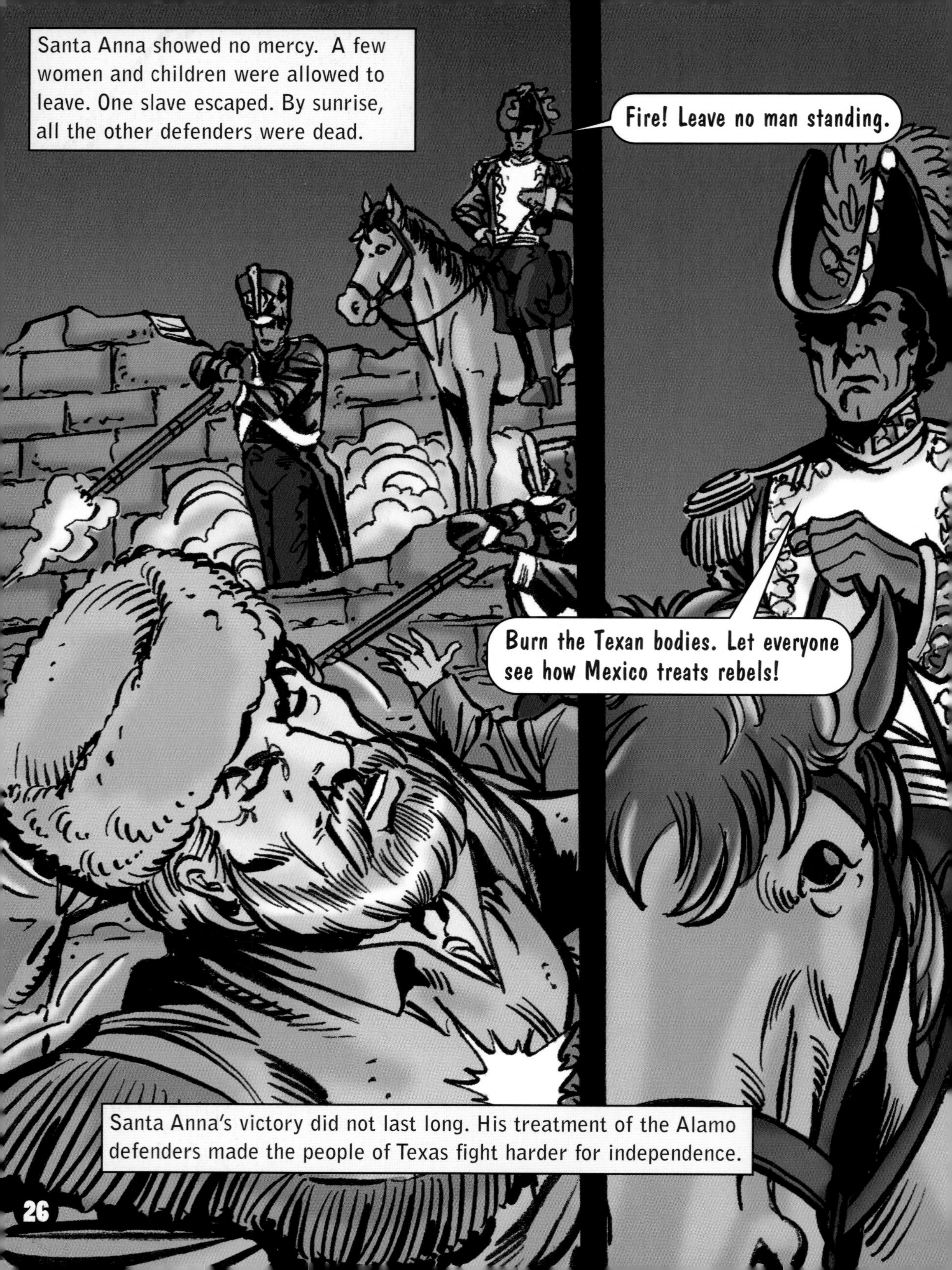
Santa Anna showed no mercy. A few women and children were allowed to leave. One slave escaped. By sunrise, all the other defenders were dead.
Fire! Leave no man standing.
Burn the Texan bodies. Let everyone see how Mexico treats rebels!
Santa Anna's victory did not last long. His treatment of the Alamo defenders made the people of Texas fight harder for independence.

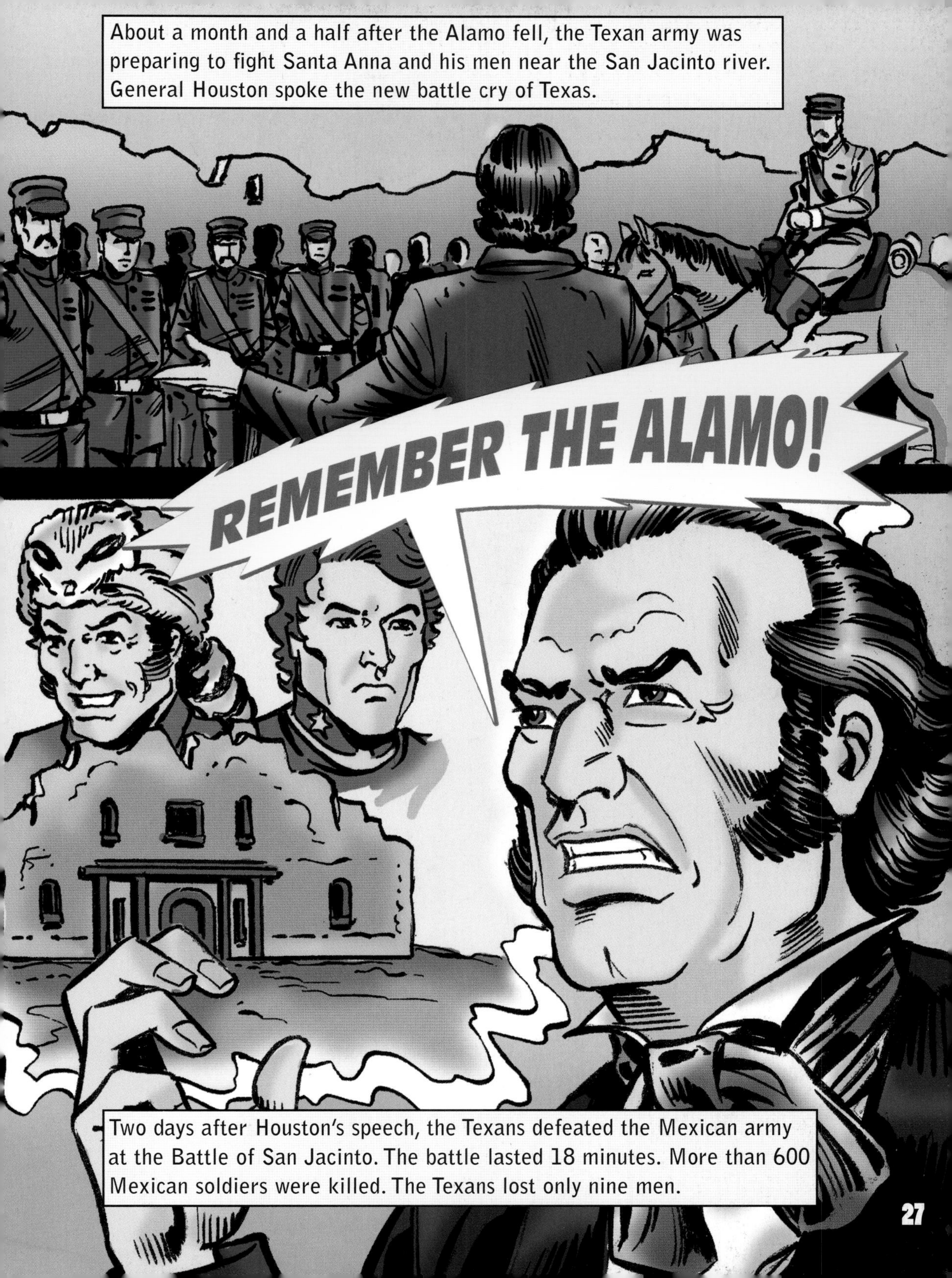
About a month and a half after the Alamo fell, the Texan army was preparing to fight Santa Anna and his men near the San Jacinto river. General Houston spoke the new battle cry of Texas.
REMEMBER THE ALAMO!
Two days after Houston's speech, the Texans defeated the Mexican army at the Battle of San Jacinto. The battle lasted 18 minutes. More than 600 Mexican soldiers were killed. The Texans lost only nine men.

MORE ABOUT ★★★ THE ALAMO

★ No one knows exactly how many people died in the Battle of the Alamo. Santa Anna reported that 600 men defended the Alamo, but most people think that the number was actually fewer than 200. Some people think that 500 or more Mexican soldiers died, but others say the number was much lower.

★ Not all of the Alamo defenders were Anglos. Some of Alamo's defenders were Tejanos. Tejanos were Hispanics who had settled in Texas.

★ Many of the Alamo defenders were not professional soldiers. They were volunteers who chose to help defend Texas. These men signed a contract when they volunteered. The contract kept them from quitting or leaving.

★ Santa Anna escaped from the Battle of San Jacinto dressed as a soldier instead of a general. He was captured the next day.

★ The Alamo was built in 1718 as a mission for American Indians who had converted to Christianity. More than 80 years later, it became a military fort.

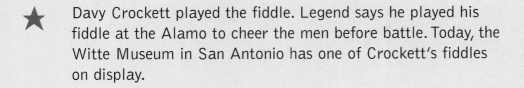 Davy Crockett played the fiddle. Legend says he played his fiddle at the Alamo to cheer the men before battle. Today, the Witte Museum in San Antonio has one of Crockett's fiddles on display.

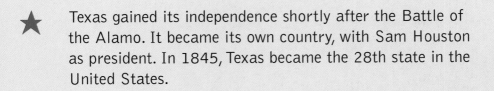 Jim Bowie was a frontiersman from Louisiana. He was famous for the large knife he carried and used in battles. Bowie knives are named for him.

William Travis was only 26 years old when he died defending the Alamo.

Texas gained its independence shortly after the Battle of the Alamo. It became its own country, with Sam Houston as president. In 1845, Texas became the 28th state in the United States.

GLOSSARY

Anglo (ANG-lo)—a white settler from a U.S. state or territory

barracks (BA-ruhks)—the part of a fort where soldiers sleep

fort (FORT)—a building that is well defended against attacks

legend (LEJ-uhnd)—a story handed down from earlier times

ruthless (ROOTH-liss)—cruel and unconcerned about others

siege (SEEJ)—an attack designed to surround a place and cut it off from supplies or help

surrender (suh-REN-dur)—to give up or admit defeat

volunteer (vol-uhn-TIHR)—someone who is not a professional soldier but offers to fight with an army; Colonel Jim Bowie led the volunteers assigned to the Alamo until he got sick; Crockett and his 12 men were volunteers from Tennessee.

INTERNET SITES

FactHound offers a safe, fun way to find Internet sites related to this book. All of the sites on FactHound have been researched by our staff.

Here's how:

1. Visit *www.facthound.com*
2. Type in this special code **0736838325** for age-appropriate sites. Or enter a search word related to this book for a more general search.
3. Click on the **Fetch It** button.

FactHound will fetch the best sites for you!

READ MORE

Bankston, John. *Antonio López de Santa Anna*. Latinos in American History. Bear, Del.: Mitchell Lane Publishers, 2004.

Burgan, Michael. *The Alamo*. We the People. Minneapolis: Compass Point Books, 2001.

Gaines, Ann. *The Alamo: The Fight over Texas.* Proud Heritage. Chanhassen, Minn.: Child's World, 2003.

Winders, Richard Bruce. *Davy Crockett*. The Legend of the Wild Frontier. New York: Power Plus Books, 2003.

BIBLIOGRAPHY

The Alamo in San Antonio, Texas. http://www.thealamo.org.

Daughters of the Republic of Texas Library. http://www.drtl.org.

Davis, William C. *Three Roads to the Alamo: The Lives and Fortunes of David Crockett, James Bowie, and William Barret Travis.* New York: HarperCollins, 1998.

Hardin, Stephen L. *Texan Iliad*. Austin, TX: University of Texas Press, 1994.

Long, Jeff. *Duel of Eagles: the Mexican and U.S. Fight for the Alamo.* New York: Morrow, 1990.

Murphy, Jim. *Inside the Alamo.* New York: Delacorte Press, 2003.

Texas A&M Digital Library. http://dl.tamu.edu/projects.html.

Texas State Library and Archives Commission. http://www.tsl.state.tx.us/treasures/republic/alamo-01.html.

INDEX